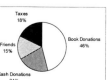

USBORNE PARANORMAL GUIDES

# ALIEN ABDUCTION?

## Philippa Wingate

### Designed by Stephen Wright

### Illustrated by Gary Bines

Consultants: John and Anne Spencer

Additional Illustrations by
Chris Keppie, Jeremy Gower and Kevin Lyles

Additional design help by
Andrew Dixon, Russell Punter
and Michael Wheatley

Series Editor: Felicity Brooks

Picture research by Ruth King

# CONTENTS

# CLOSE ENCOUNTERS

A recent survey in America revealed that 26 per cent of Americans believe that they have seen an Unidentified Flying Object (UFO). That is 90 million people. Thousands of people claim to have been actually abducted by aliens. By this they mean they have been kidnapped and taken on board flying saucers. So can you really be sure it won't happen to you?

If you do come across an alien, it is known as a close encounter. If you just see a UFO it's called a close encounter of the first kind. If the UFO leaves a mark, like a burn on the ground, it is an encounter of the second kind. In an encounter of the third kind, you actually meet an alien. The fourth, and most scary kind, is alien abduction.

## Fact or fiction?

Thousands of UFO sightings are reported every year. Many are studied by enthusiasts called UFOlogists. They spend their time searching for evidence of Extra Terrestrial life, which means life beyond our planet.

Most sightings turn out to be nothing more than an aircraft, the Moon or weather balloons.

But, to this day, over 200,000 sightings remain unexplained, and the witnesses involved remain convinced that they have encountered aliens. Some people think that the kind of person who sees a UFO has an over-active imagination; but can so many people be mistaken?

## Case studies

This book contains eight case studies. In each study there is an account of a famous close encounter, based on eye witness reports. Each account is followed by an assessment, in which the facts of the story are examined in an attempt to discover what really happened.

## Don't panic!

It is very hard to prove conclusively whether aliens are visiting our planet. In the end, it is up to you to decide what you believe. If, when you have read this book, you feel that there is strong evidence to suggest that aliens do actually exist – don't panic! If they are here, they have probably been visiting our planet for centuries, and they haven't harmed us yet.

**Are aliens visiting Earth in spacecraft that can travel faster than the speed of light?**

# Case study one: FLYING SAUCERS

Date: **June 24th, 1947**
Time: **3:00pm**
Place: **Cascade Mountains,
Washington State, USA**
Witness: **Kenneth Arnold**

## THE EVENTS

$5,000 was a very tempting reward. All Kenneth Arnold had to do was locate the wreckage of a Marine Corps C-46 plane that had gone down near Mount Rainier with 32 men on board.

Kenneth was an experienced amateur pilot and his plane was specially designed for flying in mountainous areas. On the spur of the moment he decided to spend an hour or two searching. Holding the aircraft steady at 2,750m (9,200ft), he began to scan the mountains below.

Kenneth Arnold beside his plane

### A bright light

When his initial fly-past revealed nothing, Kenneth turned back to take a closer look. But as the plane wheeled around, he was momentarily blinded by a tremendously bright light.

The flash must have been the sun reflecting off a nearby aircraft, he told himself. Frantically, Kenneth searched the sky for its source, scared that he might collide with the other plane. But the sky was empty. Maybe his mind was playing tricks on him. He opened the plane's window to look again more carefully.

### Strange craft

Off to the left, another flash lit up the sky. Whatever was causing it was moving incredibly fast. Then Kenneth saw them; nine bright objects flying just north of Mount Rainier.

### Unearthly speed

He strained his eyes to get a better look. They had to be over 30km (20 miles) away. Using the second hand on his wristwatch, he timed how long it took the shining objects to fly from the peak of Mount Rainier to Mount Adams.

**Nine craft flashed across the path of Kenneth Arnold's plane.**

The Cascade Mountains, where Kenneth Arnold spotted the nine UFOs

He had a rough idea of how far this was, and could do a quick calculation: 2,750km/h (1,700mph). Impossible. There wasn't an aircraft yet invented that could reach that speed, and it wasn't just the speed that amazed him. As the strange craft crossed his flight path, Kenneth could see that their wings were curved, shaped like boomerangs, and they didn't appear to have tails. They were darting around, flipping up and down, yet remaining in a perfect formation. As they moved, an eerie light flashed from their surface.

Were they aircraft secretly being tested by the US Air Force? Or were they some sort of guided missile? After only two and a half minutes, the craft disappeared, heading south over Mount Adams.

# Case study one: Flying saucers

## Back to base

Eager to tell someone what he had witnessed, Kenneth Arnold made for the Yakima Airfield. He landed there at approximately 4.00pm and made a report to Al Baxter, the General Manager, before flying on to the airfield at Pendleton, Oregon.

By the time he touched down, a swarm of newspaper and radio reporters was waiting for him.

## Flying saucers

Reluctantly, Kenneth jumped down from the cockpit of his Callair plane to face a barrage of questions. One reporter pushed his way forward eagerly, wanting to know exactly how the craft had moved.

Kenneth Arnold later wrote a book about the UFOs called *The Coming of the Saucers*.

Hesitating for only a moment, Kenneth told him that they had skimmed through the sky "like a saucer would if you skipped it across the water". Later, a reporter for *The East Oregonian* remembered Kenneth's words and coined the phrase "flying saucers". Little did he know that this was a name that would stick.

### The COMING of the SAUCERS

$2.50

**By Kenneth Arnold & Ray Palmer**

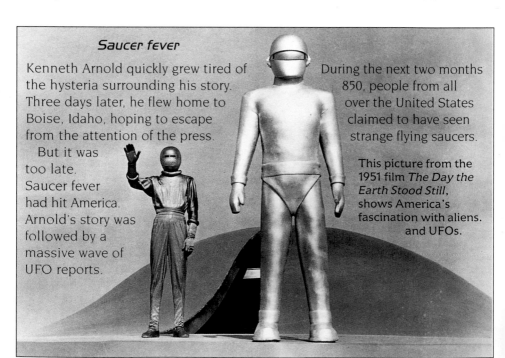

## Saucer fever

Kenneth Arnold quickly grew tired of the hysteria surrounding his story. Three days later, he flew home to Boise, Idaho, hoping to escape from the attention of the press.

But it was too late. Saucer fever had hit America. Arnold's story was followed by a massive wave of UFO reports.

During the next two months 850, people from all over the United States claimed to have seen strange flying saucers.

This picture from the 1951 film *The Day the Earth Stood Still*, shows America's fascination with aliens. and UFOs.

# Case study one: THE ASSESSMENT

The objects Kenneth Arnold spotted in 1947 were never officially identified, but here are some of the possible explanations:

A Republic XP-84 Thunderjet

### Mirages
The air over mountains often forms layers of different temperatures. When light passes through the layers, it distorts and creates shimmering images of nearby objects. These images are called mirages. Kenneth Arnold could have seen a mirage of the Cascade peaks.

### Earth lights
Mount Rainier is a dormant volcano. This means that the Earth's crust beneath it contains cracks called fault lines. When pressure builds up below the Earth's surface in these areas, it can cause bursts of energy, known as earth lights which appear as flashes of light in the air above.

### Missiles
If the objects that Kenneth Arnold saw were nearer than he thought, they would have been moving more slowly than he calculated. This means they could have been guided missiles. Missiles were regularly fired from a test range 112km (70 miles) northeast of Yakima at Moses Lake.

Guided missiles in a launcher

### Aircraft
No aircraft in use in 1947 could reach the speeds Kenneth Arnold calculated for the UFOs. Republic XP-84 Thunderjets could travel at speeds of 605mph (975km/h). Yet there is no evidence that these aircraft were being flown in the area at the time of the sighting.

### Jellyfish
Kenneth Arnold later came to believe that he had seen an unknown species of animal that lives in the stratosphere. Some UFOlogists claim these creatures exist and that they can alter their shape, like jellyfish. They argue that there are millions of undiscovered species on Earth, including ones that live in the air.

### A flock of birds
If Arnold had mistaken the distance of the objects, he would have mistaken their size, so they could have been birds. White feathers reflect light, though they are unlikely to cause a bright flash.

**Date: January 7th, 1948**
**Time: 1:35pm**
**Place: Godman Field near Fort Knox, Kentucky, USA**
**Witness: Captain Thomas Mantell Jr.**

## THE EVENTS

The Chief of Police wanted to know what on earth was going on. All day long he had been inundated with reports of UFOs. The people of Maysville, Kentucky had jammed his telephone lines with tales of a huge object floating silently through the sky. When quizzed, most of them described something that was shaped like a parachute, over 75m (250 ft) wide, and looked like it was made of metal.

### Looking for answers

At 1:15pm, the Chief of Police picked up the phone and called the nearby airbase at Godman. Could the US Air Force give him any information about the strange phenomenon that was alarming the townspeople?

His inquiry was relayed to the Air Force Test Center at Wright-Patterson Airfield. But the Air Force insisted that no aircraft fitting that description was being tested in the area. People must simply be imagining things.

### Registering on the radar

Imaginary or not, at 1:35pm radar scanners in the Godman Flight Control Tower picked up an unidentified craft approaching from the southeast at a height of 3,950m (13,000ft). Minutes later, airmen down on the runway spotted something too.

Flight Control Tower radar operator

### UFO sighted

It was clearly no ordinary aircraft. Even though they scrutinized it through binoculars, the men couldn't identify it. The object hovered motionless above the airfield for a full half hour, glowing with an eerie red light. Then it shot up into the clouds before stopping again.

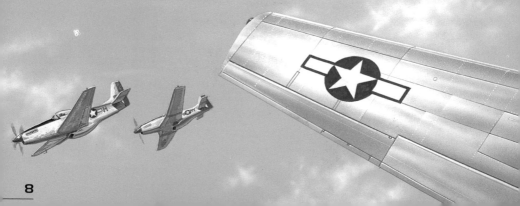

## Mustangs investigate

**Captain Thomas Mantell**

Suddenly, over the radio at the Godman Tower, came the voice of 25-year-old Captain Thomas Mantell. He was leading a flight of four P-51 Mustang fighters. Reporting their position as 16km (10 miles) south of Godman, Mantell asked the Tower's permission to fly over the airfield.

The Tower radioed back: the Mustangs were to alter their course and check out the UFO. With his excitement obvious in his voice, Captain Mantell acknowledged the new instructions and changed his course.

## A deadly pursuit

One of the Mustangs was low on fuel and had to land immediately. The remaining three began to climb, attempting to intercept the mysterious craft. At 6,700m (22,000ft) Captain Mantell's two remaining pilots gave up the chase. US Air Force regulations demanded that oxygen must be used by pilots flying over 4,200m (14,000ft) to prevent breathing difficulties, and none of the Mustangs was equipped with oxygen. Before they broke off pursuit, the pilots tried to warn Captain Mantell he was flying dangerously high without oxygen, but he flew on, climbing to 7,000m (23,000ft).

As two pilots turned back toward the airbase, Captain Mantell's P-51 Mustang continued to climb toward the UFO.

# Case study two: MANTELL'S FATAL FLIGHT

### Newspaper report

Several newspapers later reported that Captain Mantell had radioed Godman Tower with the following words: "It's fantastic! It's right above me, and it's tremendous! It looks metallic, and it's huge and circular. It could be anything between 500 and 1,000 feet across. It seems to be cruising at about 200 knots, and I'm gaining on it. It's colossal! I'm going to try and get above it. It's climbing! It's starting to climb... God, this is fantastic! It's getting hot. It's hot! The heat! I can't..."

This account is typical of how UFO stories can be exaggerated and sensationalized in newspaper reports. All that Captain Mantell actually said before his radio went dead was that he had spotted the UFO above him, that it was large and metallic, and he was gaining on it.

### A terrible end

These were the last words Captain Mantell ever transmitted. He was found two hours later. A search party came across his Mustang crashed into a field outside Franklin, Kentucky. It had exploded on impact. Inside the cockpit, they found Captain Mantell's body. His watch had stopped at 3:18pm. The search team decided that this must have been the time of the crash.

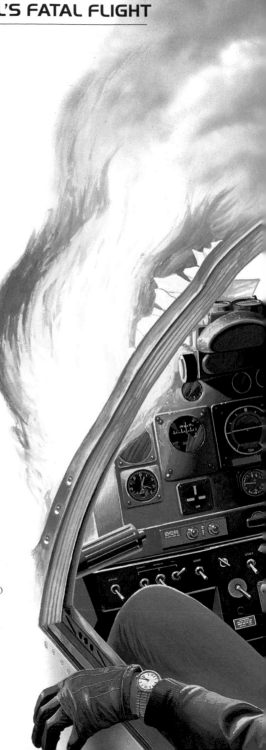

## Official statement

Almost immediately, stories began to circulate that Captain Mantell's plane had been shot down by the UFO. The US Air Force were forced to issue a statement. Captain Mantell had died when his P-51 Mustang aircraft had broken up in midair as a result of flying too high. They claimed that Captain Mantell had been chasing nothing more than the planet Venus, which had appeared strangely magnified in the sky as a result of rare weather conditions.

Captain Mantell's body was found inside the cockpit of his P-51 Mustang.

The planet Venus is the object most commonly mistaken for a UFO. It is responsible for 27 per cent of sightings.

## A change of story

Realizing that nobody believed this explanation, the Air Force soon released another statement. This time they claimed that Captain Mantell had died while chasing a weather balloon. For over 30 years, this remained the official explanation of the fatal flight.

# Case study two: THE ASSESSMENT

Many strange and exaggerated stories grew up around Captain Thomas Mantell's death. Some were prompted by the Air Force releasing misleading statements; others were caused by sensational newspaper reports.

### Chasing Venus

The US Air Force's original statement that Captain Mantell had been chasing Venus was an unlikely explanation. On a sunny afternoon it would have been very difficult to see the planet. In addition, Venus wouldn't have been picked up by the radar at Godman Tower, nor would it have been described by witnesses as a large metal object moving close to the Earth.

### Listening devices

In 1985, the Air Force changed their story again. They admitted that Captain Mantell was chasing a Skyhook balloon. The balloons had been secretly released by the US Navy from Camp Ripley in Minnesota, and were floating over the area. They were huge, 135m (450ft) tall and 30m (100ft) across, and matched the descriptions given by witnesses at Godman. The balloons were carrying equipment being used to listen into radio transmissions around the world.

Huge balloons were used to lift equipment.

### Too little oxygen

Stories quickly began to circulate that Captain Mantell had in fact been killed by a "death ray" fired from the UFO. Yet a medical examination of his body proved that he had been killed by the impact of his plane hitting the ground. Flying above 6,700m (22,000ft) without an oxygen supply, Captain Mantell would have suffered from a condition called anoxia. This means his brain was deprived of oxygen, resulting in unconsciousness. His plane would have continued to climb, out of control. Eventually, the engine would have cut out due to lack of oxygen, causing the plane to crash.

### Following orders

Captain Mantell was a very experienced pilot. This fact raises the question: why did he break the rules and fly too high without oxygen?

An intelligence officer working for the US Air Force at the Pentagon has since admitted that, during this period, Air Force pilots had been given a set of secret orders. The orders stated that if a UFO was sighted, they were to capture it at any cost. These orders may help to explain Captain Mantell's relentless pursuit of the UFO.

# IDENTIFIED FLYING OBJECTS

Thousands of UFO sightings are reported every year. After investigation, UFOlogists agree that almost 95 per cent of these can be explained by natural or man-made objects. Once a UFO has been identified, it is called an IFO (an Identified Flying Object).

### Mistaken identity

The most common objects mistaken for UFOs are stars, the planet Venus, the lights of aircraft, weather balloons and satellites. Up to 5 per cent of reported UFOs turn out to be the Moon.

### Look again

Here are just some of the things that people have mistaken for UFOs.

The photograph below appears to show a fleet of UFOs. In fact it shows a collection of clouds called lenticular (lens-shaped) clouds. They occasionally form when air rises above hills.

Lenticular clouds often look as if they are made of metal.

Ball lightning is another very rare phenomenon which can confuse observers. The lightning usually appears as a sphere of glowing light, about 20cm (8in) across.

The lightning crackles as it rolls slowly across the sky and the spheres can last for several minutes.

Ball lightning photographed at Sankt Gallenkirch, Austria, in 1978

### Bizarre explanations

Some explanations of UFOs can be very strange. One investigation concluded that a shining UFO was really an owl that had eaten fungi that glowed in the dark.

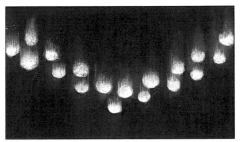

An alien spacecraft over Lubbock, Texas?

A UFO reported in Lubbock, Texas in 1951, was probably a flock of geese. The city lights reflected on the underside of their white bodies.

In 1966, the crew of Gemini 11 photographed a UFO in space. Years later it was identified as a Russian satellite, Proton-3, which burned up 36 hours after the astronauts saw it.

# Case study three: SCORCHED EARTH

**Date: January 8th, 1981**
**Time: 5:00pm**
**Place: Trans-en-Provence, France**
**Witness: Renato Nicolai**

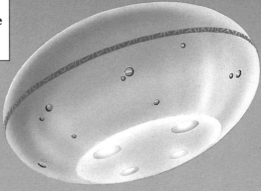

The egg-shaped craft hovered above Renato's head before it sped off.

## THE EVENTS

Renato's back was beginning to ache. He had been working hard for hours, building a water pump on his land. The land stretched down a steep hillside to a river.

At first Renato Nicolai thought that he was imagining the strange, high-pitched whistling. He was tired. Then he realized the noise was coming from above him. He glanced up from his work just in time to see a bizarre metallic-looking object landing near the foot of the hill.

### An oval craft

The craft was oval-shaped, with four small openings in its base. It came to rest gently on the ground beside an old shed.

Angry that someone was messing around on his land, Renato strode down the hill, and approached the object.

But before he got very close, the whistling sound grew louder, and suddenly the craft rose into the air. Once it was above the height of the trees, it shot off in the direction it had come from.

### Leaving traces

Renato ran to the place where the craft had landed. Imprinted on the ground was a curious circular mark. He decided he should call the police from the nearby village of Draguignan.

## Crack team

After studying the landing site, the police took photographs and collected soil samples. They soon decided they should call in GEPAN, an organization set up by the French government in 1977 after a wave of UFO sightings. Its scientists researched any reported sightings.

The GEPAN team arrived in Trans-en-Provence and began an extensive study.

## Taking samples

Samples of soil and vegetation from both inside and outside the landing area were gathered. They were sent to laboratories in Toulouse for testing. The results proved astonishing.

## Stones smashed

Where the craft had touched the ground, the earth was crushed, as if a very heavy weight had struck it. Flints in the soil had been smashed and the soil had been compressed into a hard crust. Under the microscope, the top of the crust looked as if it had been polished with sandpaper.

The soil inside the landing area contained inexplicably high levels of certain chemicals which were not present in the surrounding soil. The scientists were also amazed to discover that the soil and vegetation inside the circular mark had been heated to an incredibly high temperature, between 300°C and 600°C (570-1110°F).

## Strange findings

The scientists also tested levels of chlorophyll, the green chemical which is found in plants. The plants collected inside the landing area had chlorophyll levels that were half of those measured in the vegetation outside. It was as if the plants inside the ring had somehow mysteriously undergone extreme ageing.

## No explanations

Many researchers visited Renato's land, but all of them remained baffled. They were convinced that something had landed on the terrace, but none of them could explain exactly what.

# Case study three: THE ASSESSMENT

This is an unusual case, because thorough scientific investigations are rarely carried out after a UFO sighting. But despite the investigation the evidence it produced is inconclusive.

This egg-shaped miniature helicopter fits the description of the UFO given by Renato Nicolai better than any other craft.

### Ball lightning
The UFO may have been ball lightning, which would have scorched the earth in the 10 seconds that the UFO remained in contact with the ground. However, the appearance of ball lightning doesn't match the description given by Renato Nicolai.

### Circular craft
If the object was a man-made machine, it must have been a top-secret, experimental craft. There are few known circular craft that have ever flown successfully or stably, and there are none that would create the strange effects recorded at the UFO's landing site.

This flying saucer, called the Avro Avrocar, was built and tested in the 1950s. The project was not a success and was abandoned.

### Military activity
GEPAN checked with air traffic controllers and discovered that on January 8th, 1981, there wasn't any military activity in the area that could explain the UFO.

### Fraud
It is unlikely that the sighting was a hoax. Renato Nicolai had little to gain from inventing the UFO story, apart from local fame. Furthermore, it would have been difficult for him to create the strange effects seen at the landing site. After examining Renato, a psychologist concluded that he really believed that he had seen a UFO.

### New tests
In 1989, the plant samples taken by GEPAN from the landing site at Trans-en-Provence were re-examined using a newly developed electron microscope. The test showed that man-made chemicals, such as some kind of weedkiller, had not been responsible for the scorching marks found on the ground.

US AIR FORCE

# CROP CIRCLES

Crop circles are large circles, or collections of circles, which appear in fields. They are formed when the stems of a crop, such as wheat, are bent over at their base. The stalks lie down flat, making neat, regular patterns.

These crop circles appeared in a field at Alton Barnes, Wiltshire, UK, in July 1990.

## What causes crop circles?

Nobody knows exactly what causes crop circles, though many bizarre explanations have been offered. Some people think that they are evidence of UFO landings, or aliens sending messages through symbols drawn in fields. Alternative theories range from secret weapons testing to ball lightning. Some people think that animals, such as hedgehogs or badgers, cause the patterns by trampling down crops.

The most popular theory was put forward by Dr. Terence Meaden, a professor of Physics. He claims that a crop circle is caused by a tiny whirlwind, called a vortex, produced when certain geographical and weather conditions are combined.

## Dr. Meaden's theory

1. On a hot, calm day, wind blowing across a hill lifts up as it passes over the hill.

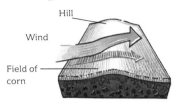

2. The wind then travels across the top of the stationary air on the other side of the hill. This creates a spinning column of air, called a vortex.

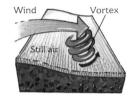

3. The moving air in the vortex causes electricity to build up inside the column. The vortex begins to rise. The electricity it contains glows, and produces a high-pitched noise.

4. If the vortex touches the ground it causes a spinning force which flattens the corn. The vortex can lift up and fall again, causing several circles to form.

## Are crop circles a hoax?

Many crop circles may be man-made. In 1991, Doug Bower and Dave Chorley admitted creating many of the circles which appeared in England in the 1980s.

To form the circles, they used two planks of wood, each attached to a piece of string. Placing their feet on the planks and holding the strings at waist height, they walked in circles, treading down the crops. To ensure they made perfect circles, they tied a piece of string to a post to guide them.

# Case study four: BESIEGED

Date: August 21st, 1955
Time: 7:00pm
Place: Sutton Farm, Kelly, near
Hopkinsville, Kentucky, USA
Witness: Multiple witnesses

## THE EVENTS

Something was out there. The dog was howling and barking wildly. Lucky Sutton thought it must be a stranger approaching the farmhouse. The dog wouldn't act like that if it was a friend.

The house was full that evening. The Sutton family were entertaining their friends Billy Ray and June Taylor. In all there were eight adults and three children who would witness the horrors the night was to bring.

At 7:00 pm, Billy Ray came in from the yard, claiming he had seen a bright object land in a dried-up riverbed nearby, but no one believed him.

### Lucky investigates

Now, an hour later, it seemed that something really was wrong. Lucky Sutton decided to go outside and investigate. His friend Billy Ray went with him. Both men took their guns, just in case.

Outside in the yard, they looked around to see what was upsetting the dog. In the distance, across a field, they caught sight of a strange light, gradually approaching the farm.

As the light came closer, the men were amazed by what they saw. It was a creature, only 1m (3ft) tall.

It had a hairless head, large yellow eyes and huge, flapping ears. It held its long, thin arms over its head as though it was surrendering. But strangest of all, it was glowing, as if lit from inside by a silvery light.

### Shoot first

Terrified, the men sped back to the farmhouse. Cowering in the doorway, they fired at the creature. It was thrown back, somersaulting through the air into the darkness. Billy Ray and Lucky realized the bullets had ricocheted off the being, as if it were made of metal.

They rushed into the house and threw their combined weight against the door to keep it shut. As they panted, trying to catch their breath, they heard one of the children scream.

### A silvery claw

The men ran into the kitchen, and saw a hideous alien face staring in at the window. Lucky fired, and the thing disappeared into the gloom.

Bullets ricocheted off
the grotesque
creature's body.

Sure that this time the creature was dead, Billy Ray went to check the body. As he stepped onto the porch, a silvery claw reached down from above the door. Horrified, Lucky rushed forward and dragged Billy Ray back into the house.

### On the roof

Everybody listened in stunned silence, as above their heads, they heard scratching and scampering. Reloading his gun, Lucky stormed outside and blasted at a creature on the roof. As the bullet hit, the alien glowed more brightly, yet seemed unharmed. Lucky felt his panic rising. They were besieged; surrounded. There were creatures everywhere.

# Case study four: BESIEGED

## Retreat

Realizing that their guns were useless against these things, the men ran back into the house and bolted the door.

For three hours everyone inside waited for the nightmare to end. They sat rigid with fear, as the aliens peered in at them through the windows.

## Making an escape

By 11:00pm they couldn't take any more. They decided to make a run for it. On the count of three, everyone burst out of the door and ran to the cars parked outside. Without looking back, they sped the 16km (10 miles) to Hopkinsville and piled into the police station.

The families left the house surrounded by aliens.

## Police investigate

Although he found Lucky's tale hard to believe, Chief of Police, Russell Greenwell, called his deputy and four other officers and drove to the farm.

A careful search of the area turned up nothing out of the ordinary – no bodies, no UFOs in the riverbed, and no glowing creatures. But there were bullet holes all over the walls of the house and buried in the dirt in the yard. Something had really scared the Suttons and their friends.

## Guns drawn

The fear was infectious. When a police officer stepped on the tail of the Sutton's pet cat, it let out an ear-piercing screech. In a split second, all the police officers had drawn their guns.

At 2:15am, Chief Greenwell decided there was nothing his men could do. They left, promising to return in the morning. Convinced the creatures had gone, and totally exhausted by their ordeal, the Suttons went to bed.

### A sleepless night

In the silent hours of the morning, Lucky's mother, Glennie, lay awake. Suddenly, she became aware of a eerie glow lighting up her bedroom. Looking over at the window, she saw an alien staring in at her.

Calmly, Glennie called Lucky, who rushed in. She begged him to leave the creature in peace, but he took aim and fired at it. The creature just floated to the ground and scampered off.

Suddenly Lucky's mother saw a grotesque face at the window.

### No answers

Nobody got any more sleep that night. The family remained prisoners in the farmhouse, watching the creatures moving around outside. But the next morning the creatures were gone, and they never reappeared.

# THE ASSESSMENT

The incident at Sutton Farm is one of UFOlogy's most extraordinary stories. There are, however, very few possible explanations of what actually happened on that night.

### Circus monkeys

Some people have suggested that the aliens were really monkeys that had escaped from a circus which had recently passed through Hopkinsville. However, no monkeys were reported missing from the circus and, anyway, monkeys are not resistant to bullets.

### A hoax

The Suttons may have invented the story to gain fame and fortune. They did put up a poster outside the farm asking for payment from people who wanted to look around, but they claimed that this was to prevent people from invading the farm. On the other hand, there are three key reasons why it is unlikely they made the story up. First, the Suttons suffered from the publicity surrounding events. Lucky's brother John lost his job, and local people were hostile to them.

Second, Lucky's mother Glennie was a very trustworthy witness. One researcher who interviewed her commented that she was the kind of person who could not tell a lie, even if her life depended on it.

Finally, the Suttons could have made money by going to the newspapers and retracting the story. Yet they have stuck to their claims for over 40 years.

# Case study five: ALIENS IN THE DESERT

Date: July 2nd, 1947
Time: 9:50pm
Place: The Foster Ranch, near
Corona, New Mexico, USA
Witness: Multiple witnesses

## THE EVENTS

An ear-splitting explosion rang out
across the desert. Just
thunder, thought sheep
rancher Mac Brazel, as he
stood on the porch of the
Foster Ranch. Yet he still
felt uneasy as he watched
the stormy night sky.

The next day Mac rode
out to check on his flock.
As he paused at the top
of a hill to the wipe
sweat from his forehead,
he suddenly noticed
below him something
glittering in the sunlight.
A trail of wreckage littered
the valley floor. It looked like
the remains of a plane.

The crash site 120km
(75 miles) northwest of
Roswell, 32km (20 miles)
southeast of Corona

### Gossip in town

Three days later, Mac went into the
town of Corona for a drink. In the bar,
he heard some customers talking
about UFOs. Apparently several local
people had reported seeing
mysterious objects speeding across
the sky. Mac wondered whether the
strange debris he had found in the
desert might be a UFO. He
decided to go to the Sheriff's
office to report his findings.

### Major Marcel investigates

The Sheriff rang Roswell
Airbase, who immediately
sent an Intelligence Officer
named Major Jesse Marcel to
go into the desert with Mac
and investigate the wreckage.

What Major Marcel found
was unlike anything he had
ever seen before.

Kneeling on the sand, he examined pieces of the debris. They appeared to be made of some kind of very light metal, like foil. There were little rods with symbols on them. When Jesse tested the debris, he found it couldn't be cut or burned. If he crumpled it up, it returned to its original shape.

### Another strange discovery

Meanwhile, 290km (180 miles) southeast, Grady Barnett stood rigid with terror. While working in the desert, Barnett had come across a strange disk-shaped aircraft that had crashed into a hillside. Strewn around the craft were the bodies of its crew. He moved closer,to get a better look. But what he saw made him freeze with horror.

### A strange crew

The four bodies were abnormally thin, with big hairless heads, large eyes and small, slit-like mouths. They were only 1.4m (4ft 6in) tall. Their arms were long and their hands had only four fingers. They were definitely not human.

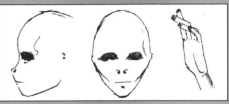

Walter Henn drew pictures of the aliens from a description given by someone who claimed to have seen their bodies.

The crashed saucer and its strange crew found by Grady Barnett

# Case study three: ALIENS IN THE DESERT

### Enter the army

Before Barnett could explore farther, a US Army jeep roared up and a troop of soldiers descended on the crash site. They had been alerted by a pilot who had seen the damaged saucer from the air. One officer told Barnett to leave immediately and to tell no one about what he had seen. The soldiers sealed off the area until they had removed every trace of the debris.

That night, transporter planes flew out of Roswell Airbase under heavy guard, taking the crash wreckage to Wright-Patterson Airbase in Ohio.

### Alerting the press

At noon the next day, an Information Officer at Roswell Airbase issued a statement which sent local newspapers crazy with excitement: a flying saucer had been found in the desert outside Corona.

Major Marcel posed for the press with debris from a weather balloon.

Hours later, the airbase issued a new statement. The saucer story was a mistake. The crash debris was only a weather balloon. Reporters were invited to examine the fragments.

### Held in isolation

Meanwhile, soldiers were sent to take Mac Brazel into custody. He was held in isolation, safely kept away from press reporters. The only statement he was allowed to make was to confirm the Army's new story.

Nobody knows what threats were made to ensure Mac never talked of what he had seen in the desert. But after his release, he didn't even discuss it with the members of his own family.

The *Roswell Daily Record* reported the UFO story

## New investigations

For 30 years the events at Roswell were pretty much forgotten. Then, in 1978, they caught the attention of a UFOlogist named Stanton T. Friedman, who launched a detailed investigation of his own. He traced 200 people who had witnessed some aspect of the incident. Several witnesses said that they had seen the four aliens retrieved from the saucer. One even claimed to have watched autopsies performed on the bodies at Roswell Airbase hospital.

## A mysterious guest

A story began to circulate that one of the saucer's crew had survived the crash. Remaining alive for over a year, it was cared for in a top-secret facility. The alien finally died of an infection that would have been relatively harmless to humans, but against which its body had no natural resistance.

## An anonymous package

In 1984, there was an exciting new development in the Roswell story. Two UFOlogists received a package through the post. Inside was a roll of 35mm film. There was no clue to who had sent it.

Once developed, the film revealed a top-secret document, dated November 18th, 1952. It appeared to have been prepared for US President Dwight D. Eisenhower.

The documents confirmed that a saucer had crashed near Roswell in 1947, and that wreckage and four alien beings had been recovered.

The documents are now known as the Majestic-12 documents, because they include a letter from Harry Truman, President of the USA in 1947, to his Secretary of Defense, instructing him to proceed with a mysterious operation called Majestic-12.

## Caught on film

In 1995, sensational news broke that the British UFO Research Association had been given a piece of film that had been shot secretly during an autopsy performed on a dead alien at Roswell.

The film showed a small, humanoid alien with no hair, large eyes, tiny nose and mouth. It had six digits on each hand and foot.

Many UFOlogists believe that the Roswell film is a hoax.

The man who released it refuses to let the film be tested to confirm what year it was made, nor will he reveal the identity of the cameraman who filmed the autopsy.

**A picture from the Roswell film**

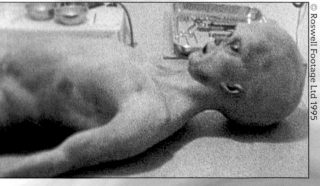

© Roswell Footage Ltd 1995

# Case study five: THE ASSESSMENT

The Roswell Incident, as it is now known, is probably the best known UFO story. Countless wild claims have been made about what really happened.

## Project Mogul

In 1994, the Air Force admitted that the balloon

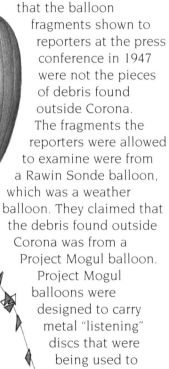

fragments shown to reporters at the press conference in 1947 were not the pieces of debris found outside Corona. The fragments the reporters were allowed to examine were from a Rawin Sonde balloon, which was a weather balloon. They claimed that the debris found outside Corona was from a Project Mogul balloon. Project Mogul balloons were designed to carry metal "listening" discs that were being used to spy on the Soviet Union.

A Rawin Sonde balloon

## Top-secret tests

It seems probable that what crashed in the desert was a top-secret device that was being tested by the government. Scientists at White Sands missile range, near Roswell, were testing thousands of pieces of military equipment at this time.

## Mystery material

Investigators believe that the strange metallic material that had so puzzled Major Marcel when he examined it may have been an early form of polyethylene. Polyethylene had indeed been invented in 1947, and it would have behaved in the manner Marcel described in his tests.

## Nuclear weapons

In 1947, the airbase at Roswell was the home base for the world's only airborne combat unit trained to handle and drop nuclear bombs. Therefore, the transport planes seen secretly leaving the airbase under heavy guard on the night of July 8th, were more likely to have contained nuclear weapons than the remains of an alien saucer.

## Crash test dummies

On June 24th, 1997, fifty years after the Roswell Incident, the United States Air Force revealed that during the 1940s, experiments were conducted in the area. Crash test dummies were thrown from high altitude research balloons. This might explain the "aliens" seen in the desert by Grady Barnett.

Dummies like these were used in government tests.

# SEARCHING FOR EXTRA TERRESTRIALS

Searching space for Extra Terrestrial beings doesn't just happen in science fiction films and books. Large sums of money are currently being spent by governments hoping to find evidence of aliens living in distant star clusters.

## Planets like Earth

The Universe is made up of huge star systems called galaxies. Each galaxy contains billions of stars, like our Sun, which have planets revolving around them. It seems likely that among these are planets with the right conditions for life to exist.

The Hubble space telescope has recently identified planets revolving around stars in a cluster called the Orion Nebula.

## Listening to space

Scientists working for a project called the Search for Extra Terrestrial Intelligence (SETI) use radio telescopes to scan space for radio signals that are repeated in a logical pattern. Such patterns would show that intelligent beings were broadcasting from another planet.

In 1974, the Arecibo dish, a huge telescope, beamed out a coded message into space. Scientists hoped that the message, which described our planet, might be picked up by distant alien civilizations.

On August 15th, 1977, SETI equipment at Ohio State Radio Observatory, USA, detected a remarkably strong radio signal. When Dr. Jerry Ehman saw the signal on a computer printout, he wrote "WOW!" next to it.

Experts don't know whether the signal was a broadcast from space, or whether they had detected a radio signal from Earth reflected off a piece of space debris. It was never recorded again, despite frequent searches.

## Receiving a reply

Several factors make the success of the SETI project unlikely. For example, the vast size of the Universe means a radio signal from Earth could take thousands of years to reach another inhabited planet. The beings living on that planet would have to have developed the technological capability of receiving, understanding and replying to the broadcast.

(Above) The creature from the film *Predator* is a typical example of Hollywood's idea of an alien being.

(Inset) In reality, recent pictures of life on Mars show that Extra Terrestrials may only exist in the form of microscopic bacteria.

# Case study six: TWO HOURS MISSING

Date: September 19th, 1961
Time: 3:00am
Place: Lancaster, New
Hampshire, USA
Witness: Betty and Barney Hill

## THE EVENTS

As the alien drove the long needle deeper and deeper into her navel, Betty Hill screamed.

Sitting bolt upright in bed, she realized she was having another of those terrible nightmares. This time, Betty decided, she would find out what had really happened that night two years ago to cause her such terror.

### Heading home

The night in question was September 19th, 1961. Betty and her husband, Barney, had been enjoying a much needed holiday in Canada. Warnings of a hurricane moving along the East Coast had prompted them to attempt to drive all through the night to get home to Portsmouth, New Hampshire.

That was how they found themselves heading south on Highway 3, which winds through the White Mountains.

It was Betty who first noticed the bright light up ahead. Barney said it was probably an aircraft, or even a satellite that had strayed off course.

The White Mountains, New Hampshire

## At Indian Head

As the light drew nearer, Betty
became convinced it was following
them. Just outside the town of
Lancaster, on a stretch of the road
known as Indian Head, Barney
slowed the car down, trying
desperately to make out what
was causing the bright light.
Eventually, he pulled over
and switched off the engine.

### In a trance

Taking his binoculars from the back
seat, Barney got out and walked toward
the light. It was now hovering at tree
level, only 15m (50ft) away.

Suddenly, Betty grew anxious. She
cried out to Barney to come back. But,
as if in a trance, he didn't seem to hear
her. He just kept walking into the light.

### A strange craft

Lifting the binoculars to his eyes,
Barney looked at the light. It was a disk-
shaped craft, and he could make out
a row of windows running around its
outer edge. Inside, he was sure he could
see figures staring down at him through
the lighted windows.

Then Barney panicked. He raced back
to the car and jumped into the driver's
seat. Fumbling with the ignition key, he
started the engine and sped off, not
stopping until they reached their home
in Portsmouth, New Hampshire.

Barney could see
strange figures in the
spaceship above him.

# Case study six: TWO HOURS MISSING

### Missing time

Confused and alarmed, Betty reported their experience to a local UFOlogist. When he questioned them about the evening, a disturbing fact came to light. Their journey home from Lancaster had taken far longer than it should have. Two hours were missing.

Their story, however, was just one of thousands the UFOlogist had to investigate and it went to the bottom of his pile of cases.

### Nightmares

Then the nightmares started. In her dreams, Betty was back in the car on Highway 3. She decided to seek help. She contacted a doctor in Boston, who used hypnosis on patients to find out the causes of their anxieties.

### Under hypnosis

Dr. Simon was stunned by what he heard. Under hypnosis, Betty and Barney described the events of September 19th, and their stories were frighteningly similar.

With their voices betraying their fear, they spoke of finding the highway blocked by a group of strange beings. They were not very tall, but they had large pear-shaped heads.

The track ahead of the Hills was blocked by unearthly beings.

### On board a UFO

The next thing they knew, Betty and Barney found themselves floating up out of their car and into a spaceship.

Once inside, they were subjected to a series of medical examinations, during which samples were taken from their bodies. Betty remembered the pain of a long needle that was inserted into her navel. This was the pain that had tortured her in her dreams for so many nights.

### A map of the stars

Throughout the examinations, the aliens spoke to Betty and Barney. They didn't use their mouths, but communicated with their thoughts.

After the tests, one of the creatures showed Betty a chart. He told her that the pattern of lines and dots was a star map, showing the trading routes they followed through space. He assured Betty that she wouldn't remember any of this once she had been returned to her car. She swore she would.

### Back to Earth

Somehow the couple found themselves back in their car. The UFO departed, lighting up the sky with an orange glow.

When Dr. Simon brought the Hills out of their trances, they were shocked to discover what they had recounted.

# Case study six: THE ASSESSMENT

The Hills were a highly respectable couple, who had no reason to lie about their experiences. However, an examination of the facts of the case casts doubts on their story.

Betty and Barney Hill with Barney's picture of the alien spacecraft.

### 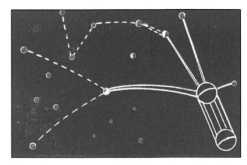 Radar report
Pease Air Force Base, whose radar covers the Indian Head area, reported tracking an unknown object in the early hours of September 19th, 1961. So there is little doubt the Betty and Barney Hill did see a UFO that night.

### Missing time
The Hills claimed they could not account for the extra two hours their journey home took. Missing time is a common experience of many people who claim to have been abducted. However, it is possible that the time the Hills spent watching the strange light, and stopping to get a closer look, may have accounted for two hours.

### Nightmares
Barney's and Betty's account of their abduction experiences were remarkably similar. However, it is probable that Betty would have described her dreams to Barney. Under hypnosis, Barney may have recounted her version of events as if he too had experienced them.

### Star map
Under hypnosis, Betty drew a copy of the star map the alien had shown her. In 1974, Marjorie Fish, an amateur astronomer, constructed another map based on Betty's. She decided that the pattern suggested the aliens came from Zeta Reticuli, a star system about 3.7 light years away from Earth.
However, Carl Sagan, a famous astronomer, used computers to study Marjorie Fish's map, and found that the Zeta Reticuli star system bore little similarity to Betty's star map.

Betty's star map, with lines showing the aliens' trade routes linking the stars

### Many sightings
After Barney died in 1969, Betty reported many encounters with aliens. As a result, many people began to doubt the truth of her original story.

# ALIEN SPACE TRAVEL

The distances that separate the planetary systems in our galaxy are vast. If aliens are visiting Earth, they have developed technological capabilities far beyond our own to make such incredible journeys possible.

### Light years away

To describe distances in our galaxy astronomers use "light years". Light is the fastest thing in the Universe. It travels at 300,000km (186,000 miles) per second, and one light year is the distance light travels in a year – 9.46 million million km (5.8 million million miles). Our galaxy is 100,000 light years across. To travel these vast distances, Extra Terrestrials would have to have developed a spacecraft that can move at the speed of light.

This is the amazing alien spaceship in a film called *Close Encounters of the Third Kind*.

### Unearthly speeds

Scientists believe that it is not possible to travel at the speed of light. However, they used to think that supersonic travel (faster than the speed of sound) was impossible, until a Bell X-1 plane flew at supersonic speeds in 1947.

The Bell X-1 plane, flown in 1947

In the future, new understanding of the physics of the Universe may enable humans to build craft that can travel at the speed of light or faster. In 1,000 years time, it may be possible to cross the Universe in minutes.

### Great journeys

Other planetary systems are light years away from Earth, so even if aliens could travel at the speed of light, their journey to Earth would take many years. In human terms, this is a long journey, because humans only live for about 80 years. But different living things have different life spans. For example, bristlecone pines in California, USA, live for nearly 5,000 years. For all we know, aliens may live for thousands of years, and could, therefore, easily undertake journeys that lasted hundreds of years.

### Shortcuts

Aliens may have discovered shortcuts through space. There may be holes or distortions in space caused by forces of gravity. These may create bridges, bringing two objects on different sides of the Universe closer together.

Date: **November 5th, 1975**
Time: **6:15pm**
Place: **Apache Sitgreaves National Forest, near Heber, Arizona, USA**
Witness: **Travis Walton**

## THE EVENTS

Once all the gear was safely stowed away in the back of the truck, Mike Rogers and his crew of six forestry workers set off through the pine forest, heading for town.

### Light ahead

Just as they reached the top of a hill, Mike slammed on the brakes. Up ahead, hovering above the ground, was a disk-shaped object.

It was over 6m (20ft) wide and 2.5m (8ft) high, and glowing with an amber light.

The crew froze with fear, all except 22-year-old Travis Walton. He scrambled down from the truck, and began to approach the UFO. As he drew closer, it began to vibrate ominously.

### Struck by a beam

Suddenly a beam of green-blue light, like a laser, shot out from the base of the hovering disk. It hit Travis, spinning him around and throwing him to the ground.

With a shriek of terror, Mike stepped on the accelerator pedal and the truck sped off along the logging track. One of the crew looked back, but he had to shield his eyes. Travis was completely enveloped by the blinding light.

**Travis was struck by a blinding ray of light from the UFO.**

## Deserters

As the truck bounced along the track, the crew sat in silent horror. They had left their friend out there; deserted him.

Mike didn't slow down until they reached the town of Snowflake. They drove straight to the Sheriff's office and told him their strange story.

## Murder suspects

Despite an intensive search, after three days the police had found no clue to the disappearance. They turned their attentions to the forestry crew. Maybe the whole story was a hoax, or even a cover-up for murder. Had the crew killed Travis and then invented the UFO story to cover their tracks?

## Search party

A full-scale search was launched immediately. The police, together with a band of volunteers, scoured the forest for Travis. Too terrified to go back, three of the forestry crew refused to join the search party. The Sheriff's men spread out along the track, peering through the trees and shouting Travis's name. When they paused to listen for a reply, all they heard was the wind and the screeching of an owl.

## Questions

Sheriff Ellison had the crew brought into the police station. Pounding his fist on the table in anger and frustration, he demanded to know where Travis's body was hidden. But the men insisted that they didn't know. They seemed genuinely upset. One man wept. Even Sheriff Ellison found it hard to believe they were just acting.

# Case study seven: KIDNAPPED BY ALIENS

### Lie detection

A polygraph machine, otherwise known as a lie-detector, was brought in. Polygraph machines register the level of stress in a subject by measuring changes in heartbeat and sweat rate. A person telling lies usually exhibits more stress than one who is telling the truth. One by one, the men were tested. Exactly what had happened on the night of November 5th?

Compiling the results seemed to take forever. Outside the Sheriff's office the crew sat in silence.

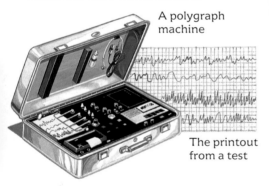

A polygraph machine

The printout from a test

Would they be arrested for murder? Or would they be free to go home?

Finally, the door of the office swung open, and Ellison came out. They were free to go. They had all passed the tests.

### A phone call

In the middle of the night, a shrill ring of the telephone woke Travis's sister from a deep sleep. She stumbled downstairs and picked up the receiver. To her amazement, she heard Travis's voice on the other end of the line.

Six days after his disappearence, there he was on the other end of the telephone, sounding confused and muddled. He told her that he was in a phone booth just outside the town of Snowflake, which was about 19km (12 miles) away.

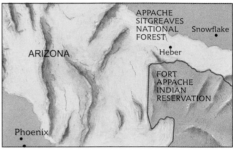

Apache Sitgreaves National Forest, Arizona

Immediately, Travis's brother jumped into his car and headed for Snowflake.

Cautiously, he approached the phone booth. He saw a strange figure huddled beside it. Drawing nearer, he realized that it was Travis; wild-eyed, bedraggled and exhausted.

### Back home

Back home and wrapped in blankets, Travis sat cowering on the sofa. His sister paced around him, firing questions: What had happened? Where had he been for so many days? Was he OK?

Taking a deep breath, Travis began to speak. As he told her his incredible story, she sat in silent amazement.

### Travis's story

Travis vividly recalled the night of November 5th. He remembered the moment in the forest when the ray of light had hit him. He must have fallen unconscious, because the next thing he remembered was lying on a table in a brightly lit room.

Painfully, he lifted his head to look around him. He decided that he must have been taken to a hospital; so he began to call for a nurse.

### Aliens on board

At that moment Travis's blood ran cold. Instead of a nurse or a doctor, three monstrous alien creatures appeared, leaning over him.

He stared aghast at their hairless heads, huge eyes, and slit-like mouths, then he bolted off the table.

**Three hideous creatures peered down at Travis.**

### Bolt for freedom

Searching desperately for a weapon, Travis seized a piece of equipment and swung it at the aliens. Visibly alarmed, they rushed out of the room.

Travis hesitated. What should he do now? Where could he go? He ran out of the room, sprinted along a corridor and into another room.

Momentarily he forgot his panic. Gazing around him, he contemplated an amazing view of the Universe, with its galaxies and stars. He realized that he was aboard some kind of craft, which was shooting through space.

### Man in a helmet

Suddenly aware of someone standing behind him, Travis spun around. A being had entered the room.

Travis could see billions of stars all around him.

It looked human, but wore a strange helmet. It motioned Travis to follow and led him out of the UFO, into a vast building, which looked like an aircraft hangar. Around him, Travis saw several more saucer-shaped craft. There were other beings there too. They were tall and blond with beautiful golden eyes.

The being in the helmet beckoned to Travis.

### Back to Earth

Travis began to question the being in the helmet: Where was he? What was happening? But instead of receiving an answer, he was told to lie down. Travis recalled a mask being placed over his face and the next thing he knew, he was standing on a highway.

With a roaring sound and a blast of heat, the UFO shot straight up into the sky and disappeared from sight.

Travis managed to drag himself to a telephone and call his sister, before collapsing in a heap.

# Case study seven: THE ASSESSMENT

Many people believe Travis Walton's abduction was a hoax. They think he may have made up his story, but they don't know why he did it.

## A broken contract

Mike Rogers' crew had a forestry contract, but they were falling behind with the schedule. With winter coming, they would have been unable to finish the job until spring. By inventing the bizarre abduction story the crew may have hoped to distract attention from their failure and to receive payment for the work they had already completed.

## A practical joker

It is important to consider that Travis Walton had a criminal record, and was a notorious practical joker. He may have come up with the idea of the hoax himself. He was very interested in UFOs and owned many books on the subject. Certainly, his mother seemed suspiciously unconcerned about her own son's disappearance. To support his claims, however, Travis Walton took a lie-detector test, which appears to confirm he really believed that he had been abducted by creatures from another planet.

## Sticking together

Any member of the crew who had decided to come forward and expose the abduction as a hoax would have been richly rewarded for his story. However, all seven men have stuck to their accounts since the day the incident took place.

## Hallucinations

Some people have suggested the forestry crew were hallucinating when they saw Travis Walton abducted. But it is unlikely that six men would have shared the same hallucination.

## Missing for five days

In the forest, Travis Walton may have been hit by a bolt of lightning. If this had knocked him unconscious, he might have lain undiscovered for five days, despite the search. This seems unlikely, however, because he would have suffered from severe exposure.

The blow may have caused Travis to lose his memory. He could have wandered around lost, or checked into a motel to recover. This is unlikely though, because despite widespread publicity about the abduction, no one reported seeing Travis Walton during the time he was missing.

Travis Walton

# WHAT DO ALIENS LOOK LIKE?

Over the years, thousands of aliens have been encountered. UFOlogists base their ideas of what Extra Terrestrials look like on the details of these sightings. Few photographs have ever been taken of aliens. Those that exist are too indistinct to give us much information about their appearance.

## A huge variety

The descriptions witnesses have given of aliens vary hugely. Red, blue, green and silver creatures have been sighted. Some beings wear robes, others wear nothing. There are aliens which are tall and heavily built, and those which are tiny and very thin. One Extra Terrestrial spotted in Venezuela was completely covered in hair, while another seen in Kentucky, USA, appeared to be made of metal.

## Real or imagined?

The great diversity in the appearance of Extra Terrestrials may indicate that witnesses are unreliable. Many encounters could be imaginary or dreams. It is also possible that people have mistaken animals or ordinary objects for aliens.

One possible explanation for different appearance of the aliens visiting Earth, is that they come from different planets. Alternatively, they could be a selection of different beings from a single planet. This isn't beyond belief. Earth has many creatures of different shapes and sizes, from elephants to ants.

This alien, seen in Scotland in 1979, was probably a land-mine.

These pictures are all based on witnesses' descriptions of alien beings.

This creature was spotted by two boys in California, USA, in 1955.

In 1958, a motorist in Niagara Falls, USA, saw two creatures with six limbs floating out of a UFO.

A farmer saw this white form in a vineyard in Spain, in 1979.

## Humanoids

Most witnesses who encounter aliens describe them as humanoid. This means that their bodies are a similar shape to that of a human being – two arms, two legs, a head with eyes, a nose and a mouth. Yet scientists think it is unlikely aliens would look like us.

The human body has developed in response to the particular environment and conditions on Earth. If, for example, Earth was twice its present size, humans would have heavier skeletons.

They would be unable to walk upright on two legs, due to the increased gravitational pull a planet that size would exert. Therefore, beings from a planet with a completely different environment from Earth's should look very different from us.

Some UFOlogists have suggested, however, that aliens can alter their appearance. They may choose to take on a humanoid shape when they come to this planet to avoid terrifying the people they meet.

This creature, with large insect-like eyes, is the most commonly encountered alien.

An alien with elephant skin and head spikes was seen in Mississippi, USA, in 1973.

This 1.80m (6ft) insect was seen by a lawyer in Maryland, USA.

Tall, blonde aliens, known as Nordics, are often described.

# Case study eight: UFO OVER NEW YORK

Date: November 30th, 1989
Time: 3:00am
Place: Manhattan Island,
New York, USA
Witness: Multiple witnesses

## THE EVENTS

Something terrible was about to happen. Linda sensed it. The hairs on her neck were prickling with fear, and a numbness crept through her body.

It was 3:00am, and Linda Cortile was in bed. Turning to her husband asleep beside her, she shook him and shouted his name – but he didn't stir.

When a small creature appeared in the doorway, Linda knew what was happening. It had happened before. She was being abducted by aliens.

A ghostly creature stood in the doorway.

### Totally paralyzed

With the last drop of energy in her body, Linda picked up a pillow and threw it at the approaching alien. But the pillow fell short of its target, and Linda could do nothing more to protect herself.

She was totally paralyzed. Thankfully, her mind went blank. When she came to, she found herself back in her room, lying on her bed.

### Signs of life

Frantic with the fear that the aliens had killed her family, Linda ran into her sons' room. The two boys were lying motionless, and didn't appear to be breathing. Linda's heart froze.

Seizing a small mirror, she held it under each of their noses in turn. Relief flooded through her as she saw the glass mist with their breath. They were in an unnaturally deep sleep – but they were alive.

### Seeking help

Linda had first gone to UFOlogist Budd Hopkins in April 1989. She wanted help. She was inexplicably certain that she had been abducted by aliens 20 years earlier.

Budd often used hypnosis to help people remember experiences of which they had no conscious memory. Sure enough, under hypnosis, Linda relived an abduction experience.

Now, only seven months after her first visit to Budd, Linda was sure that she had been abducted again.

Linda Cortile

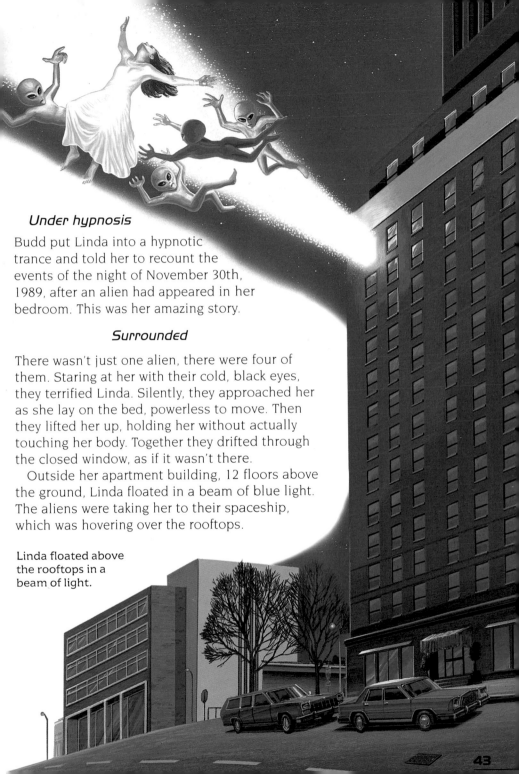

### Under hypnosis

Budd put Linda into a hypnotic trance and told her to recount the events of the night of November 30th, 1989, after an alien had appeared in her bedroom. This was her amazing story.

### Surrounded

There wasn't just one alien, there were four of them. Staring at her with their cold, black eyes, they terrified Linda. Silently, they approached her as she lay on the bed, powerless to move. Then they lifted her up, holding her without actually touching her body. Together they drifted through the closed window, as if it wasn't there.

Outside her apartment building, 12 floors above the ground, Linda floated in a beam of blue light. The aliens were taking her to their spaceship, which was hovering over the rooftops.

Linda floated above the rooftops in a beam of light.

# Case study eight: UFO OVER NEW YORK

### On board

On board the craft, Linda watched terror-stricken, as the aliens crowded around her with instruments and probes in their spindly hands. She was subjected to a terrifying medical examination. But then the next thing she remembered, she was back in her bed.

Everything was going smoothly, until they crossed Brooklyn Bridge. Suddenly the engine of the limousine they were using cut out. As they sat mystified in the silent car, both the police officers and their important passenger saw an incredible sight.

### An angel

High above them, a woman in a flowing white nightgown drifted through the night sky. Like an angel, she floated through the air and into a saucer-shaped craft. With her were three or four strange-looking creatures.

Once the group had disappeared inside the UFO, it sped away over the city, toward the East River. Without slowing down, it plunged under the surface of the water and disappeared.

### Abduction witnesses

At first, Budd didn't think Linda's story exceptional. He had heard hundreds of similar claims. But 15 months later, he changed his mind. A letter arrived at his office. It had no return address. It appeared to be from two police officers. They only signed their first names – Richard and Dan.

They wrote of an experience that had disturbed them deeply for over a year.

### On secret service

On the night of November 30th, 1989, Richard and Dan had been escorting a major political figure to New York's heliport.

Worried for the woman's safety, the police officers waited, watching the river for nearly an hour to see if she was brought back.

### More evidence

In November 1991, another startling letter arrived at Budd's office. It was from a woman who Budd calls Janet Kimble – although this is not her real name. She explained that on the night of November 30th, 1989, she had been driving across Brooklyn Bridge when her car mysteriously broke down.

The UFO plunged into the river, just beside Brooklyn Bridge.

Looking around her, Janet realized that all the lights along the bridge were out, and the other cars on the bridge seemed to have stopped too. As she got out of her car to see what was happening, Janet witnessed an amazing sight. A woman surrounded by several aliens floated into a UFO.

Mysteriously, Janet's story matched that of Linda and of the two police officers in many of its details.

### An important story

Budd realized that Linda Cortile's case might be one of the most important of all time, because her abduction had been witnessed by at least four people.

47

# Case study eight: THE ASSESSMENT

An alien abduction witnessed by several unconnected individuals is a rare occurrence. However, there are certain factors which make the stories of the four witnesses less convincing than they might appear at first.

### No witnesses

Opposite Linda Cortile's apartment block are the offices of *The New York Post*. At 3:00am, when Linda claims she was abducted, journalists were working in these offices. However, none of them saw anything unusual, let alone a woman floating outside their window.

The offices of *The New York Post*

### No names

It is suspicious that the police officers, Dan and Richard, never agreed to meet Budd nor to reveal their true identities. The men claimed to have been worried about the woman they saw abducted, yet they waited 15 months before contacting Budd Hopkins to report what they had seen.

### Power failure

In her letter, Janet Kimble described a power failure on Brooklyn Bridge which affected other motorists. This is not a common experience, yet none of the other motorists involved ever reported the incident.

### Coincidence

It seems an incredible coincidence that all the people who claim to have witnessed Linda Cortile's abduction contacted Budd Hopkins rather than another UFOlogist.

### Mystery man

Many UFOlogists suggest that the man the police officers were escorting was Perez de Cuellar, then Secretary General of the United Nations. Although there is no record of a political figure using the heliport that night, the mission was top-secret, and may not have been recorded.

The United

Senõr Perez de Cuellar

Nations insist that Senõr de Cuellar was at home in bed at 3:00am on November 30th. Perez de Cuellar himself has never spoken about the incident. If a figure of his standing did confirm that he had witnessed the abduction, this truly would be the story of the century.

# GLOSSARY

This is a glossary of unusual words you will come across in this book and other words you may see when reading further about aliens and UFOs.

**Abduction**   Being taken on board an alien flying saucer.

**Alien**   A creature not from this planet.

**Area 51**   A location in the High Desert in Nevada, USA, where top-secret technology is studied and developed by the US government. Some UFOlogists believe that flying saucers that have been found are studied there.

**Crash retrieval**   Taking the debris of crashed UFOs to examine and study. Some people believe that flying saucers that have crashed on our planet are collected by military or government organizations and studied.

**Disinformation**   The deliberate release of false information to mislead people. Some UFOlogists suspect that governments try to discredit or cover up the truth about alien encounters by broadcasting ridiculous or misleading stories.

**Earth lights**   A natural energy which experts believe is caused by stresses and strains in the Earth's crust. This energy can give off light, and might explain some UFO sightings.

**Extra Terrestrial**   Another name for an alien.

**Flying saucer**   A word used to describe UFOs that are believed to be from another planet.

**Humanoid**   An alien that is basically shaped like a human in appearance, with two arms, two legs, and a head with eyes, a nose and a mouth.

**Men In Black (MIBs)**   Sinister people who attempt to discourage witnesses from revealing details of their close encounters. Some people believe that MIBs are aliens covering up evidence of their existence.

**Missing time**   A period of time which an individual cannot account for. Many UFOlogists believe that it indicates that a person has been abducted.

**MJ-12 group**   A government organization that UFOlogists believe collects and studies flying saucers. The **MJ-12 documents** are a series of documents which seem to reveal the existence of the group.

**Project Blue Book**   The American government's UFO project which ran from 1952 to 1969, investigating any evidence of alien visits.

**UFOs** (Unidentified Flying Objects)   Unexplained objects seen by witnesses in the sky, which some people believe might be flying saucers.

**UFOlogist**   A person who studies UFOs.

# INDEX

The publishers are grateful to the following organizations for permission to reproduce their material:
(t=top, b=bottom, r=right, l=left)
p4 Fortean Picture Library; p6 (tr) Fortean Picture Library; (b) Courtesy 20th Century Fox/The Ronald Grant Archive; p8 Science and Society Picture Library/National Museum of Photography, Film and Television; p9 Fortean Picture Library; p12 Corbis-Bettmann; p13 (bl) Fortean Picture Library; (tr) Werner Burger/Fortean Picture Library; p17 Fredrick C. Taylor/Fortean Picture Library; p23 Walter Henn; p24 (bl) Fortean Picture Library; (tr) Fortean Picture Library; p25 © Roswell Footage Ltd 1995; p26 US Air Force photo; p27 (t) Courtesy 20th Century Fox/The Ronald Grant Archive; (b) Nasa/Science Photo Library; p28 With thanks to Steve Bloor, Car Magazine; p32 Fortean Picture Library; p33 (bl) Columbia Pictures/The Ronald Grant Archive; (tr) TRH Pictures; p39 Dennis Stacy/Fortean Picture Library; p 42 Dennis Stacy/Fortean Picture Library; p 46 (l) *The New York Post*; (r) Corbis-Bettmann/Reuters.
Thanks to: British UFO Research Association; Stanton T. Friedman.